RENOIR

Catherine de Duve

Have fun discovering the life and work of Renoir

KATE'ART
EDITIONS

Portraits

Family life

The Art and Life of Renoir

Small dogs

Graceful dancers

His friends at the ball

Renoir liked to paint happiness. Look at his favorite subjects. Which do you prefer?

Beautiful women

Boaters on a Sunday

Children and their games

PORCELAIN

Pierre-Auguste Renoir was born on 25th February 1841, in Limoges, central France. His father, Leonard, was a humble tailor and his mother, Marguerite, a dressmaker. He was one of seven children. The family moved to Paris in the hope of finding better work and living conditions. Renoir had a talent for art and singing. His school teacher, *Charles Gounod*, asked him to sing in the choir. But Renoir's father encouraged him to learn to paint on porcelain, a traditional craft in his hometown.

***Charles Gounod** (1818-1893) was a French composer. He composed religious arrangements and operas, including* Faust *and* Romeo and Juliet.

It's your turn to decorate this porcelain teacup and teapot, just like Renoir used to do.

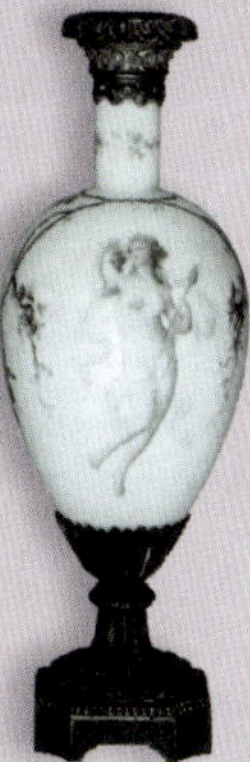

When Renoir was 13, he had to leave school to help his parents. He became an apprentice at a porcelain-decorating workshop. He painted delicate bouquets of flowers and portraits on teacups, plates and vases, as well as taking drawing classes. Soon though, the industry started using transfers instead of hand painting and Renoir was out of a job. He went on to paint fans and church banners, as well as decorating *coats of arms* for his brother. He worked quickly with great creativity.

***Coat of arms:** In the Middle Ages, families, communities, towns and corporations had their own distinctive crest (drawing), colors and motto, known as a shield, coat of arms or heraldic bearings.*

LE LOUVRE

Renoir dreamed of becoming an artist one day! A real artist! He was given permission to make copies of the magnificent pieces of art in the Louvre. How marvellous!
The works of the great masters filled room after room.

Follow in Renoir's footsteps. Stroll around museums and let the paintings inspire you.

Delacroix

He admired the voluptuous women painted by Rubens and found inspiration in the lightness and joy of paintings by Fragonard and Boucher. He was happy in this environment. He also loved Delacroix's paintings of oriental women as well as Watteau's life-size Pierrot the clown.

Rubens

Watteau

Fragonard

Boucher

ARTIST'S STUDIO

When Renoir was 21 his dream became reality as he entered the School of Fine Arts. He learned to copy and paint historical scenes. He was a diligent student but his teachers did not think him particularly talented. He also went to Swiss artist Charles Gleyre's private art studio. He met a lot of other young artists there, such as **Sisley**, **Monet*** and **Bazille**. They all became good friends.

Bazille painted his studio. Who are his friends? Who are the paintings by? Who is playing the piano?

* To find out more, take a look at *The Little Monet*, in the same collection

BOHEMIA

Portrait of Bazille painted by Renoir in 1867

The artists had a truly bohemian lifestyle! Renoir lived with Sisley, then with Bazille and Monet. "I'm delighted, I have enough room and they're both very lively," Bazille wrote in a letter to his parents. The young artists were free. School was over!

They worked together, became each other's models, and shared any models who had come to pose for one of them. For a number of years, however, life was hard for these young artists whose talent had not yet been recognized. They made postcards to earn money.

Portrait of Renoir painted by Bazille in 1867

One day, they went to the forest of Fontainebleau to paint in the open air, emulating the painters from **the Barbizon School.** There was so much more light there!

The Barbizon School

In 1848, a group of painters went to the village of Barbizon, close to **Fontainebleau forest**, and painted in the great outdoors. A first!

SALON

Renoir and his companions used to meet at the *Café Guerbois* in the Rue des Batignolles in Paris, just around the corner from their studio, to discuss "Art". Now they had to become famous. The only way was to take part in the official Salon exhibition which showcased the work of the best French artists each year. To achieve this, they had to present their canvases to a very conservative jury that did not like innovation!

Unfortunately, most of their paintings were rejected. It was so hard to make a success of things. And you still needed to earn enough to eat a square meal a day. That is why they began to show their works at the so-called "Exhibition of Rejects", a yearly event open to all, where works were judged by the public.

There was no time to lose. The artists worked on new paintings to be displayed at the next Paris Salon. The younger generation wanted to showcase a new way of painting.

Renoir presented his paintings to the jurors of the Salon. Do you agree with the jury's choice?

1879

ACCEPTED

1872 **REJECTED**

1865 **ACCEPTED**

1867 **REJECTED**

1867 **ACCEPTED**

AT THE WATER'S EDGE

Look at the painting. Would you like to have lived in those times?

Water, with its reflections and the play of light, inspired Impressionists like Monet and Renoir. The two friends went to Croissy Island. Side by side, they painted the floating cabaret of *La Grenouillère**.

Sadly, the war between France and Prussia broke out in 1870. Renoir had to join his garrison where he became very sick. His friend Bazille, a volunteer recruit, was killed in battle at the age of 29. When Renoir was finally able to return to Paris, he painted views of the city, like the Pont-Neuf that straddles the River Seine.

* To find out more, take a look at *The Little Monet*, in the same collection

THE OPERA

Who is she with tonight?

At the Opera this evening, a woman with a pale complexion is sitting at the balcony of her theatre box. She is wearing a striped dress and Belle Epoque jewelry. A multi-strand pearl necklace covers her throat, and roses are pinned to her hair. Behind her a well-dressed man observes Parisian society at its best.

Everything looks delicate in this impressionist painting. The models in this artwork are close friends of the artist: pretty Nini and Edmond, Renoir's younger brother. This canvas was sold at the first Impressionist exhibition that Renoir and his friends organized in April 1874 *.

What are the accessories you absolutely have to take with you to the opera? Find each object in the painting.

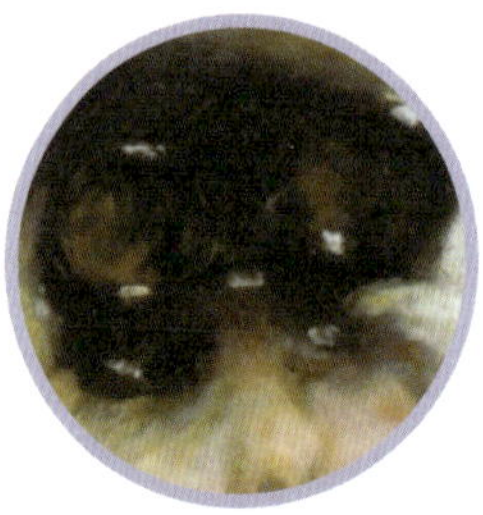

Opera glasses

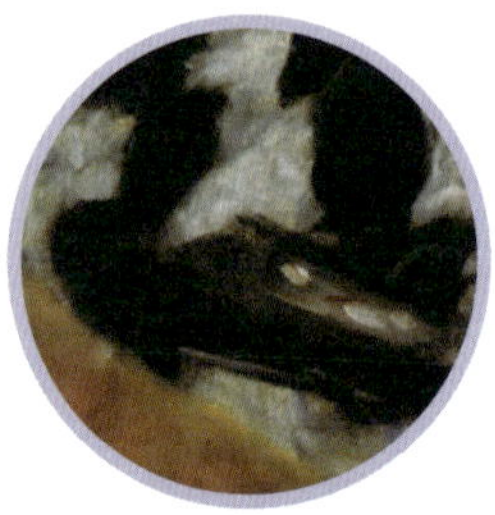

Fan

White gloves

Jewelry

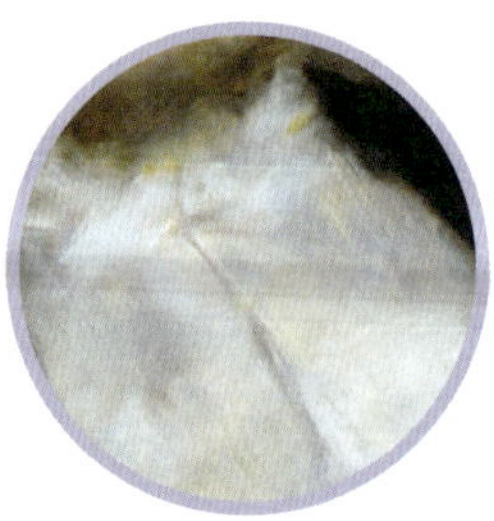

Bow ties

Roses

*To find out more, take a look at *The Little Monet* and *Long live Impressionism and Pointillism!,* in the same collection

THE MOULIN

DE LA GALETTE

Let the orchestra play, let the young people dance! This is the ball at the *Moulin de la Galette*. It is a beautiful Sunday afternoon. This local dance at Montmartre, above Paris, attracts a young crowd. Renoir's friends are regulars there. It is so lively. They dance, drink and chat. Can you hear the orchestra?

Technique

Renoir painted **vibrant touches of pure color.** The painting is bathed in an atmosphere of blue reflections. **The light** that filters through the trees highlights a couple dancing. Who are they?

Look for the pendant with the black satin ribbon in the painting. How many top hats and straw boaters can you see?

FAMILY

Madame Georges Charpentier and her children pose in a golden glow. She was the wife of a wealthy publisher who published books by Zola, Daudet and Maupassant. The lovely Saint Bernard dog looks at the artist with watchful eyes! Everything in the room seems to resonate with color.

Find the dog, the peacocks and the bird.

PORTRAIT

Life is sweet! The portrait was accepted by the jurors at the Paris Salon of 1879. Madame Charpentier used her influence to ensure that it was hung in a choice spot and it was exhibited to great acclaim.

What an opportunity for Renoir! His friend, the painter Pisarro, wrote: "Renoir has had great success at the Salon. I believe that his career has been launched. Good for him! Poverty is so hard!" Thanks to the money from this commission, Renoir was able to rent a house in Montmartre.

Richard Wagner

Renoir's portraits were very successful. He painted the celebrities of the day, such as the actress Jeanne Samary, from the *Comédie-Française*, and **Richard Wagner**, the German composer, who gave him less than an hour to paint him whilst on a trip to Sicily.

Who wrote what? Match each book or piece of music to its writer or composer:

Daudet •	• Bel-Ami
Zola •	• The Rougon-Macquart
Maupassant •	• Rhinegold
Wagner •	• Letters from my Windmill

BOATERS

Renoir has settled down on the terrace of the *Maison Fournaise* restaurant in Chatou, overlooking the River Seine and its many pleasure boats. The artist has gathered together his friends and his fiancée, **Aline Charigot**, as well as her small dog. The painter **Gustave Caillebotte** is sitting while **Alphonse Fournaise** and his sister **Alphonsine** are leaning against the guardrail. **Angèle Legault** is drinking from a glass. The actress, **Jeanne Samary**, is blocking her ears with her fingers. The painter **Paul Lhote**, dressed in red and white, and **Eugene Pierre Lestinguez**, from the Ministry of the Interior, are standing next to her. The banker **Charles Ephrussi** is wearing a top hat and talking with the poet **Jules Laforgue**, who is smoking a pipe. **Ellen André**, the actress, is wearing pearl earrings and is speaking with **Adrien Maggiolo** the journalist. There is a stranger hiding amongst them. Could it be the artist himself?

Who is who? Find the different people in the picture. How many are there?

PAUL CÉZANNE

Renoir was forever seeking to reinvent himself. He wanted to find a very personal way of painting. Thanks to the sale of his canvases, at long last he was able to travel. He took a trip to **Algeria** in 1881, following in the footsteps of the artist Delacroix. He also journeyed through **Italy** where he admired Raphael's frescoes in Rome and the paintings of Pompeii.

Provence, South of France

Upon his return he visited Cézanne and observed his approach to painting very closely, admiring his structured style, using faceted, applied strokes.

UMBRELLA

It is pouring down! The open umbrellas create a blue roof. They glint in the teeming rain. You can make out two different styles of painting in this picture. The right-hand side of the painting (1881) is typically impressionist.
Renoir has used spontaneous dashes of paint and created relief when working on the small girls, putting a lot of emphasis on light. The left-hand side (1885) clearly shows that his style has evolved. His composition is structured.

Observe the two ways in which Renoir has painted this one painting. Who's wondering whether it's still raining?

Impressionist touches

Neat outlines

Smooth paint

Flat brushstrokes

THE PIANO LESSON

After the rain comes the sun! In 1892 Renoir exhibited 110 canvases at the Gallery Durand-Ruel in Paris. They were received to great acclaim. *Young Girls at the Piano* was his first work of art to become part of a national collection and established his fame the world over. Renoir made four versions of this painting, his technique forever evolving. His style became more fluid, the colors more transparent. This was Renoir's "pearly period".

Match the details to the text and fill in the missing words.

It's time for the .... lesson. Two young girls decipher a .... What are they playing? One of them has golden .... a dress with pearly reflections and blue .... She tinkles on the piano whilst the other .... accompanies her.

CLOWNS

F**ernando Circus** was on Boulevard Rochechouart in Paris. Artists like Degas, Renoir, Toulouse-Lautrec, Seurat and Picasso came to have fun and to find inspiration. The funniest clown in Paris, **Gerónimo Medrano**, performed here. "Boom, Boom!" He laughs out loud at the conductor. He is wearing an outfit with embroidered butterflies and flowers and his face is completely white! He is wearing a funny powder puff wig. Children loved him because he made them laugh without scaring them.

They had three sons, **Pierre** (1885), **Jean** (1894) and **Claude** (1901). "It's not easy to model for Daddy". This is what's going through the mind of the eight-year-old model.

Who is this small clown in the baggy costume? He looks like Pierrot!

It's Coco, Renoir and Aline's youngest son.

JUGGLERS

The supporting artists have just finished their juggling act in the circus ring, and while one of them picks up the orange balls, the other takes a bow.

How many balls are there? Do you know how to juggle? With 2, 3, 4, 5 balls?

CAGNES-ON-SEA

The Renoir family moved to the warmer climate of the **South of France** in 1900, settling at *Les Collettes*, a farm in Cagnes, in 1907. It was bliss painting amongst the olive trees bathed in the Mediterranean sun!

The artist hoped that the mild climate would help alleviate the terrible rheumatism in his joints and the arthritis that was badly deforming his hands. Poor Renoir! Despite bouts of paralysis and suffering broken arms he continued to paint. He had to have his paintbrushes tied to his misshapen hands. He made sculptures together with Richard Guino, a young sculptor, who followed his orders, and in a way, became his hands.

Coco's Head, 1908

Imagine... If you had to paint happiness, what would you paint?

THE BATHERS

Renoir liked to paint women, nudes, joy and freedom.
They bathe, splash each other and rest, nymph like, in a heavenly setting where youth, happiness and effervescence appear to be timeless.

Who are these bathers?
How many are there?
Where are they?
Do you find them pretty?

Renoir spent three years of his life working on a large painting, *The Bathers*. Did he seek inspiration from Cézanne and the old masters who had painted them too? Before going to work on this painting he made a lot of preliminary drawings. Renoir sought composition and clear lines, unlike the new ways of painting, such as *Cubism*. *The Bathers* was to be the culmination of his life's work and the source of inspiration for many great painters such as **Picasso** and **Matisse*** who could admire this painting.

Cubism: Around 1907, the artists Picasso and Braque invented a new way in which to represent reality. They painted the same object from different angles, all on the same canvas. The most famous painting from this period is Picasso's *The Young Ladies of Avignon**.

*To find out more, take a look at *The Little Picasso* and *The Little Matisse*, in the same collection

Record

During his lifetime, Renoir completed approximately 6,000 works of art. An absolute record for an artist!

Pierre-Auguste Renoir died in Cagnes-On-Sea on 3rd December 1919 at the age of 79.
He was and still is one of the most famous French painters.

Text and illustrations: Catherine de Duve
Graphic design: Kate'Art Editions
Adaptation into English: Kerry-Jane Lowery and Rachel Beasley

Renoir: PARIS: Musée d'Orsay: *The Swing*, 1876: cover, p.32 – *Torso, sun effect*, c. 1875-1876: p. 3 – *Ball at the Moulin de la Galette*, 1876: p. 3, 16-17 – *Frédéric Bazille paintingt at his easel*, 1867: p. 9 – *Portrait of William Sisley*, 1864: p. 10 – *Portrait of Richard Wagner*, 1882: p. 19 – *The Bathers*, 1918-1919: p. 30-31 – **Musée national de l'Orangerie:** *Young Girls at the Piano,* 1892: cover, p. 24-25 – *Claude at play*, c. 1905: p. 2 – *The Clown (Claude Renoir)*, 1909: p. 26 – **Private Collection:** *Portraits of Children by Martial Caillebotte*, 1895: p. 3 – *Head of Coco,* bronze, 1908: p. 29 – **LONDON: Courtauld Institute Galleries:** *The Lodge*, 1874: p.14-15 – **National Gallery:** *The Umbrellas*, c. 1881-1885: p.23 – **BERLIN: Staatliche Museen zu Berlin-Preussischer Kulturbesitz, Nationalgalerie:** *Children's Afternoon at Wargemont*, 1884: p.1, p. 2 – **ESSEN: Folkwang Museum:** *Lise with a Parasol*, 1867: p. 11 – **OTTERLO: Kröller-Müller Museum:** *Clown in the Circus*, 1868: p. 26 – **NEW YORK: The Metropolitan Museum of Art:** *Portrait of Madame Charpentier with her Children*, 1878: cover, p. 10, p. 18-19 – **WASHINGTON, D.C: Phillips Collection:** *The Boat Party Lunch*, 1880-1881: cover, p. 20-21 **National Gallery of Art**: *Girl with a Hoop*, 1885: p. 2 – *Head of a Dog*, 1870: p. 3 – *La Dancer*, 1874: p. 3 – *Diana the Huntress*, 1867: p. 11 – *The Pont-Neuf*, 1872: p. 13 – **MERION (PA), The Barnes Foundation:** *Jeanne Durand-Ruel*, 1876: cover – **DETROIT (MI), Detroit Institute of Arts:** *The White Pierrot (Jean Renoir),* 1901-1902: p. 26 – **CHICAGO: Art Institute of Chicago:** *At the Circus Fernando*, 1879: p.27 – **CAMBRIDGE (MA): Fogg Art Museum, Harvard University Art Museums:** *Self-portrait at Age 35,* 1876: p. 4 – **PORTLAND (OR): Portland Art Museum:** *The Seine at Argenteuil*, 1873: p. 2 – **TOKYO: Bridgstone Museum of Art, Ishibashi Foundation**: *Terraces in Cagnes*, 1905: p. 28 – **National Museum of Western Art, Matsukata Collection**: *Interior of a Harem in Montmartre (Parisian Women Dressed as Algerians)*, 1872: p. 11
Others: PARIS: Musée d'Orsay: Bazille: *The Artist's Studio rue de la Condamine*, 1870: p. 8 – *Portrait of Renoir*, 1867: p. 9 – Cézanne: **USA.: The Cleveland Museum of Art:** *Mont Sainte-Victoire*, 1904: p. 22 – **Louvre:** Boucher: *Diana Leaving her Bath*, 1742: p. 7 – Delacroix: *Women of Algiers in Their Apartment*, 1834: p. 6 – Watteau: *Gilles (Pierrot)*, c. 1713-1721: p. 7 – Fragonard: *The Bathers*, before 1756: p. 7 – Rubens: **MUNICH: Alte Pinakothek, Bayrische Staatsgemäldesammlungen:** *Helena Fourment with her Son Francis*, 1660-1664: p. 6
Photographs: *Vase*, 1857: p.5 – *Pierre-Auguste Renoir*, c. 1860: p. 8 – *Renoir at his easel in front of the Villa de la Poste in Cagnes-on-Sea*, 1903: p.31 – © Fotolia: pp. 2-7, pp. 16-17, p. 20

With thanks to: Dorine Devosse, Priscilla d'Oultremont, Daniel de Duve and Joséphine Vanderborght, Véronique Lux and all those who contributed to the creation of this book.